PIANO FOR BEGINNERS

LEARN TO PLAY

CLASSICAL MUSIC

THE ULTIMATE BEGINNER PIANO SOLO SONGBOOK WITH 50 FAMOUS CLASSICAL PIECES BY MOZART, BACH, BEETHOVEN, CHOPIN, TCHAIKOVSKY, BRAHMS, SCHUBERT, AND MORE

Producer & International Distributor
eBookPro Publishing
www.ebook-pro.com

Piano for Beginners - Learn to Play Classical Music
Piano Made Easy Press

Copyright © 2022 Made Easy Press

All rights reserved; No parts of this book may be reproduced or transmitted in any form or by any means, electronic or mechanical, including photocopying, recording, taping, or by any information retrieval system, without the author's explicit permission in writing.

Transcribed by Seyapianist

Contact: agency@ebook-pro.com

CONTENTS

LEVEL 1 — 9

Ave Maria by Johann Sebastian Bach — 10

Lullaby by Johannes Brahms — 11

Canon in D by Johann Pachelbel — 12

Joy To The World by George Frideric Handel — 13

Impromptu No. 3 by Franz Schubert — 14

Italian Song by Pyotr Ilyich Tchaikovsky — 16

Liebestraum No. 3 by Franz Liszt — 18

Minuet in G Major by Johann Sebastian Bach — 20

Ode to Joy by Ludwig van Beethoven — 21

Minute Waltz from *Opera La Boheme* by Frederic Chopin — 22

Nocturne in E flat Major by Frederic Chopin — 24

Prelude from *Opera Carmen* by Georges Bizet — 26

Spring from *the Four Seasons* by Antonio Vivaldi — 27

Summer from *the Four Seasons* by Antonio Vivaldi — 28

Waltz No. 2 by Dmitri Shostakovich — 30

Wedding March by Felix Mendelssohn — 32

LEVEL 2	**35**
Arabesque No. 1 L. 66 by Claude Debussy	36
Arietta by Edvard Grieg	38
Can-Can by Jacques Offenbach	39
Eine Kleine Nachtmusik by Wolfgang Amadeus Mozart	40
Gymnopedie No. 1 by Erik Satie	42
Humoresque by Antonin Dvorak	44
In The Hall Of The Mountain King by Edvard Grieg	45
Little Prelude in G minor by Johann Sebastian Bach	46
Minuet in A minor by Henry Purcell	47
Musette's Waltz from *Opera La Boheme* by Giacomo Puccini	48
Reverie by Claude Debussy	49
Rondo Alla Turca by Wolfgang Amadeus Mozart	50
2nd movement from Pathetique Sonata by Ludwig van Beethoven	51
Sonata in C Major by Wolfgang Amadeus Mozart	52
Swan Lake by Pyotr Ilyich Tchaikovsky	54
Venetian Boat Song by Felix Mendelssohn	56

LEVEL 3	**59**
Bolero by Maurice Ravel	60
Caprice No. 24 by Niccolo Paganini	61
Clair de Lune by Claude Debussy	62
Fur Elise by Ludwig van Beethoven	64
Habanera from Opera *Carmen* by Georges Bizet	65
Hungarian Dance No. 5 by Johannes Brahms	66
Moonlight Sonata by Ludwig van Beethoven	68
Nessun Dorma from the Opera *Turandot* by Giacomo Puccini	70
Nutcracker March by Pyotr Ilyich Tchaikovsky	71
Piano Concerto No. 1 by Pyotr Ilyich Tchaikovsky	72
Piano Concerto No. 2 by Sergei Rachmaninoff	74
Prelude in C Major by Johann Sebastian Bach	75
Predule in E minor by Frederic Chopin	76
Rhapsody in Blue by George Gershwin	77
Symphony No. 5 by Ludwig van Beethoven	78
The Blue Danube Waltz by Johann Strauss II	80
Toccata and Fugue in D minor by Johann Sebastian Bach	82
Waltz in A-flat Major by Johannes Brahms	83

INTRODUCTION

50 famous piano classics for beginners to master!

With **50** of the world's most famous solo piano pieces by composers such as Mozart, Bach, Beethoven, Chopin, and many more, these shortened and simplified versions of the timeless classics are an easy first step into the world of piano.

Divided into three separate levels of difficulty, this book will allow you to slowly learn and graduate to more complex pieces of music, at your own pace and time.

From Swan Lake to the Wedding March, Clair de Lune and opera arias, discover the amazing and beautiful world of classical music right at your fingertips.

Level 1

Ave Maria

Simplified & shortened version

Arr. Daniela Diaconu

Comp. Johann Sebastian Bach

Brahms' Lullaby
Simplified & shortened version

Arr. Daniela Diaconu Comp. Johanness Brahms

Canon in D
Simplified version

Arr. Daniela Diaconu
Comp. Johann Pachelbel

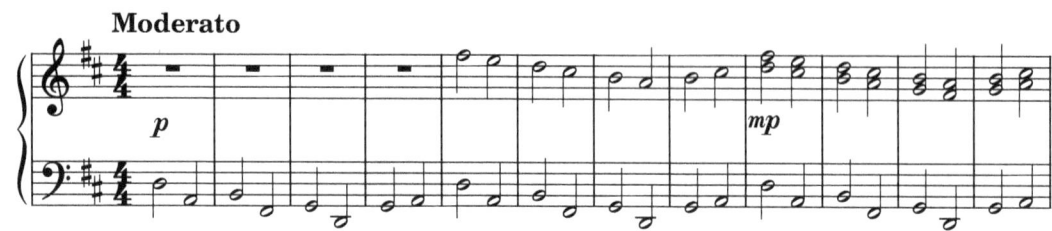

Joy To The World
Simplified & transposed version

Arr. Daniela Diaconu Comp. George Frideric Handel

Impromptu No. 3
Simplified & transposed version

Arr. Daniela Diaconu
Comp. Franz Schubert

Italian Song
Simplified & transposed version

Arr. Daniela Diaconu

Comp. Pyotr Ilyich Tchaikovsky

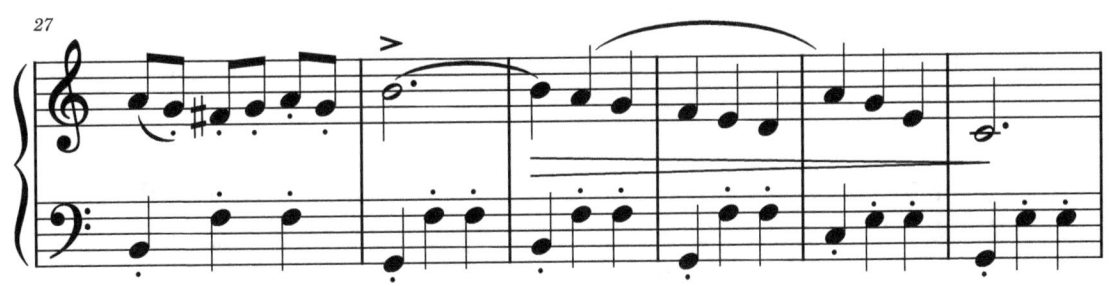

Liebestraum No. 3
Simplified & transposed version

Arr. Daniela Diaconu

Comp. Franz Liszt

Minuet in G Major
Simplified version

Arr. Daniela Diaconu

Comp. Johann Sebastian Bach
Attributed to Christian Petzold

Ode to Joy
Simplified & shortened version

Arr. Daniela Diaconu

Comp. Ludwig van Beethoven

Allegro

Minute Waltz
Simplified and transposed version

Arr. Daniela Diaconu

Comp. Frederic Chopin

Nocturne in E flat Major
Simplified & transposed version

Arr. Daniela Diaconu
Comp. Frederic Chopin

Prelude from Opera *Carmen*

Simplified & shortened version

Arr. Daniela Diaconu

Comp. Georges Bizet

Allegro Giocoso

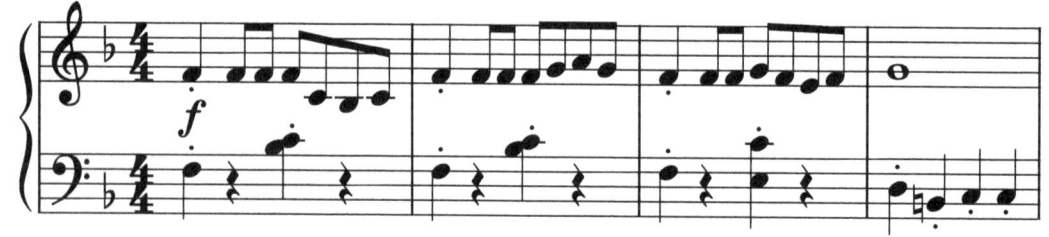

Spring
from the *Four Seasons*
Simplified & transposed version

Arr. Daniela Diaconu
Comp. Antonio Vivaldi

Summer
from the *Four Seasons*
Simplified & transposed version

Arr. Daniela Diaconu

Comp. Antonio Vivaldi

Allegro non molto ♩ = 70

Waltz No. 2
Simplified & transposed version

Arr. Daniela Diaconu

Comp. Dmitri Shostakovich

Wedding March
from *Midsummer Night's Dream*
Simplified version

Arr. Daniela Diaconu

Comp. Felix Mendelssohn

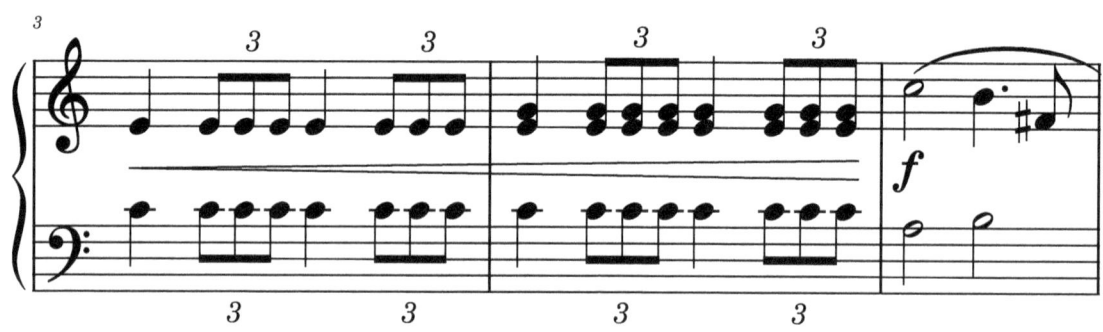

Level 2

Arabesque No. 1 L. 66
Simplified and transposed version

Arr. Daniela Diaconu

Comp. Claude Debussy

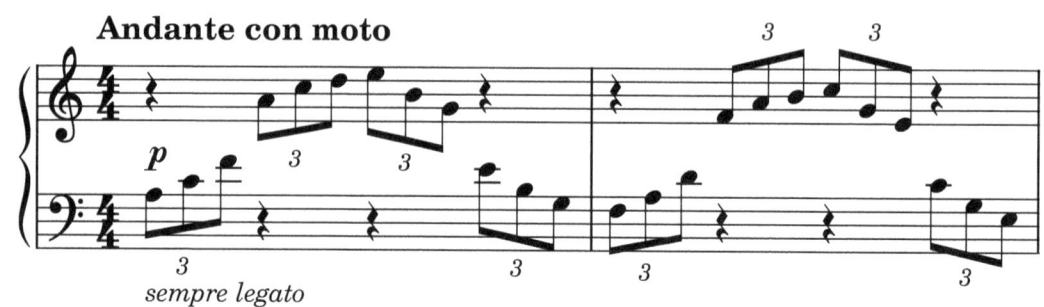

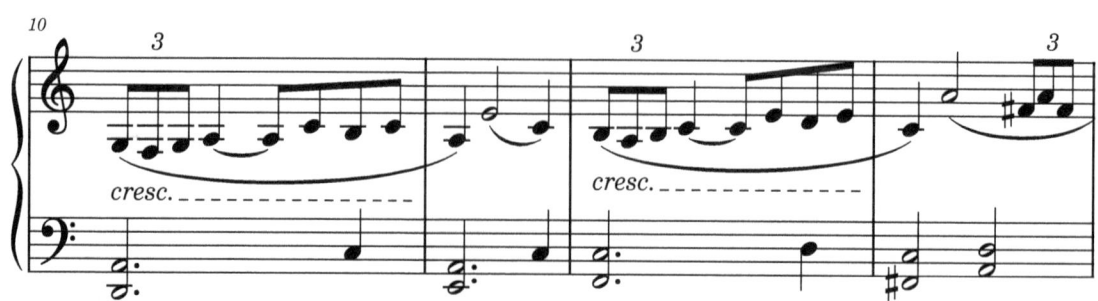

Arietta

Simplified and transposed version

Arr. Daniela Diaconu

Comp. Edvard Grieg

Can-Can

from *Orpheus in the Underworld*

Simplified & transposed version

Arr. Daniela Diaconu

Comp. Jacques Offenbach

Eine Kleine Nachtmusik
Simplified & transposed version

Arr. Daniela Diaconu

Comp. Wolfgang Amadeus Mozart

Gymnopedie No. 1
Simplified and transposed version

Arr. Daniela Diaconu

Comp. Erik Satie

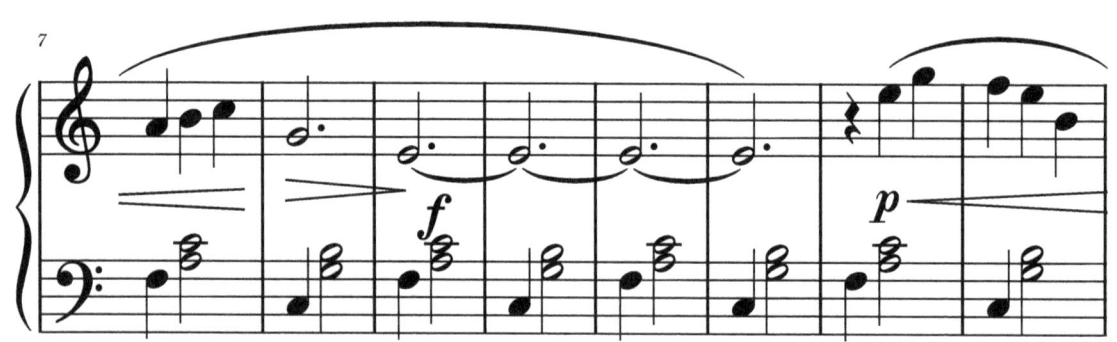

Humoresque
Simplified & transposed version

Arr. Daniela Diaconu

Comp. Antonin Dvorak

In The Hall Of The Mountain King

Simplified & transposed version

Arr. Daniela Diaconu Comp. Edvard Grieg

Alla marcia e molto marcato

45

Little Prelude in G minor
Simplified & shortened version

Arr. Daniela Diaconu

Johann Sebastian Bach

Minuet in A minor
Simplified version

Arr. Daniela Diaconu

Comp. Henry Purcell

Musette's Waltz
from Opera *La Boheme*

Simplified & transposed version

Arr. Daniela Diaconu

Comp. Giacomo Puccini

Reverie

Simplified & shortened version

Arr. Daniela Diaconu

Comp. Claude Debussy

Rondo Alla Turca
Simplified version

Arr. Daniela Diaconu

Comp. Wolfgang Amadeus Mozart

Second Movement from Pathetique Sonata
Simplified & shortened version

Arr. Daniela Diaconu
Comp. Ludwig van Beethoven

Sonata in C Major
Simplified version

Arr. Daniela Diaconu

Comp. Wolfgang Amadeus Mozart

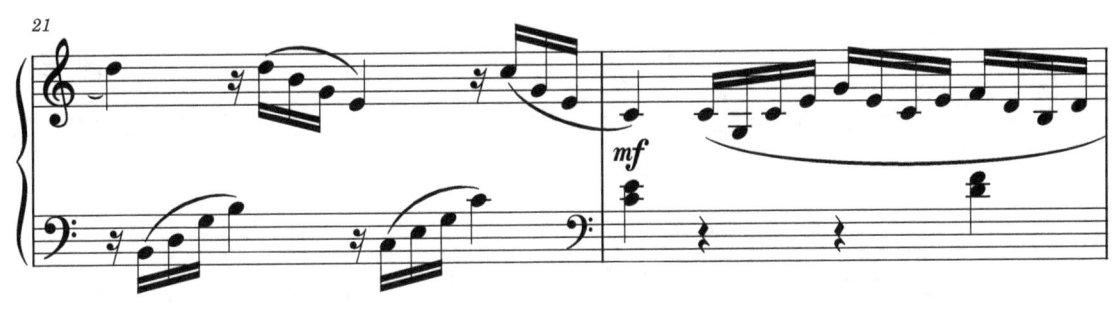

Swan Lake
Simplified & transposed version

Arr. Daniela Diaconu Comp. Pyotr Ilyich Tchaikovsky

Venetian Boat Song
Simplified

Arr. Daniela Diaconu

Comp. Felix Mendelssohn

Level 3

Bolero
Simplified version

Arr. Daniela Diaconu
Comp. Maurice Ravel

Paganini Caprice No. 24
Simplified version

Arr. Daniela Diaconu

Comp. Niccolo Paganini

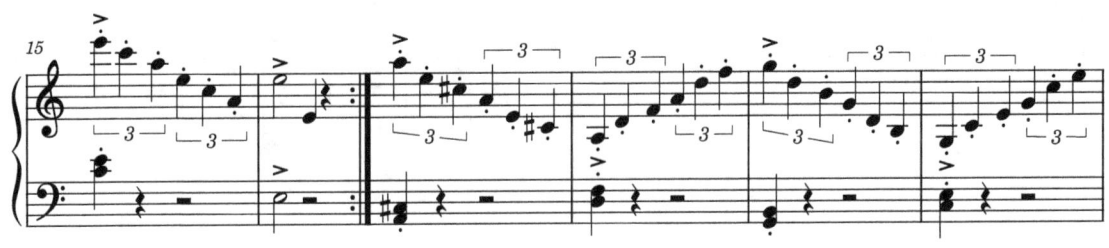

Clair de Lune
Simplified and transposed version

Arr. Daniela Diaconu   Comp. Claude Debussy

Andante tres expressif

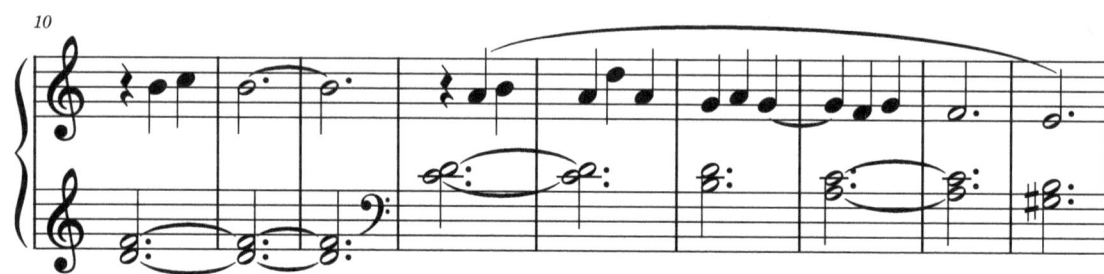

Fur Elise
Simplified & shortened version

Arr. Daniela Diaconu

Comp. Ludwig van Beethoven

Habanera from opera *Carmen*
Simplified & shortened version

Arr. Daniela Diaconu

Comp. Georges Bizet

Hungarian Dance No. 5
Simplified & shortened version

Arr. Daniela Diaconu
Comp: Johannes Brahms

Moonlight Sonata
Simplified & shortened version

Arr. Daniela Diaconu

Comp. Ludwig van Beethoven

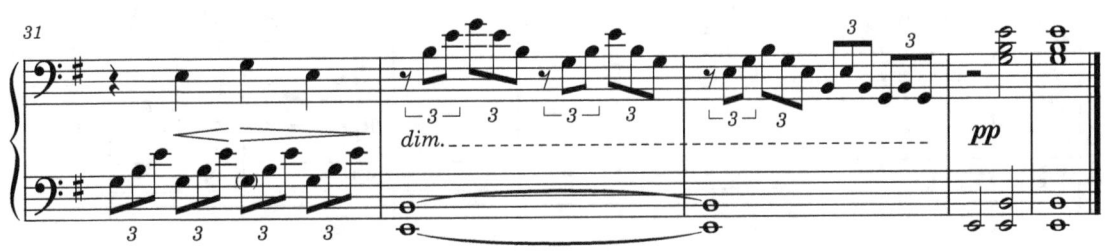

Nessun Dorma
from the Opera *Turandot*
Simplified version

Arr. Daniela Diaconu

Comp. Giacomo Puccini

Nutcracker March
Simplified and transposed version

Arr. Daniela Diaconu

Comp. Pyotr Ilyich Tchaikovsky

Piano Concerto No. 1
Simplified version

Arr. Daniela Diaconu

Comp. Pyotr Ilyich Tchaikovsky

Piano Concerto No. 2
Second movement
Simplified & transposed version

Arr. Daniela Diaconu Comp. Sergei Rachmaninoff

Prelude in C Major
Simplified & shortened version

Arr. Daniela Diaconu

Comp. Johann Sebastian Bach

Predule in E minor
Simplified version

Arr. Daniela Diaconu

Comp. Frederic Chopin

Rhapsody in Blue
Simplified & transposed version

Arr. Daniela Diaconu

Comp. George Gershwin

Symphony No. 5
Simplified & shortened version

Arr. Daniela Diaconu

Comp. Ludwig van Beethoven

Allegro con brio

The Blue Danube Waltz
Simplified version

Arr. Daniela Diaconu　　　　　　　　　　　　　　　　　　　　　　　　　　　　Comp. Johann Strauss II

Tempo di Valse ♩ = 170

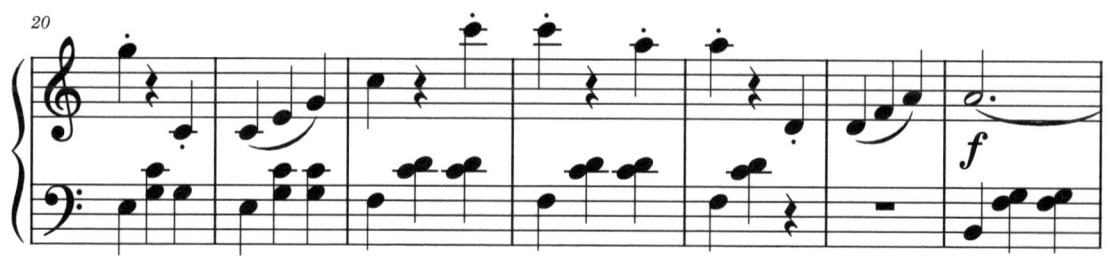

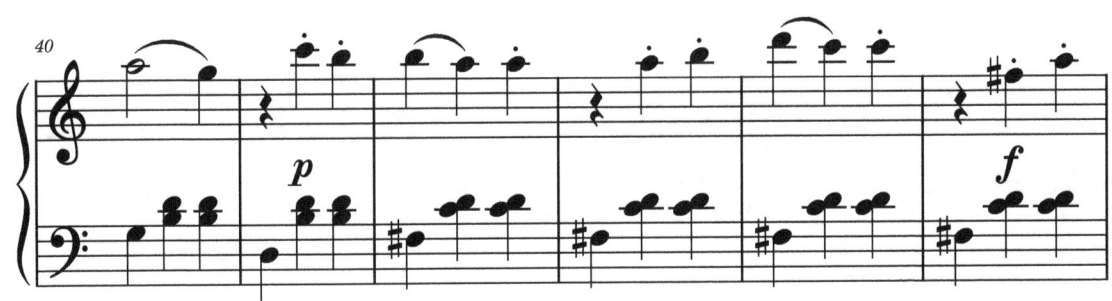

Toccata and Fugue in D minor
Simplified & shortened version

Arr. Daniela Diaconu Comp. Johann Sebastian Bach

Waltz in A-flat Major

Simplified & transposed version

Arr. Daniela Diaconu

Comp: Johannes Brahms

We hope you enjoyed this book and that it inspired in you a true love for music!

It would be so great if you could rate us on Amazon and leave a review, it means so much and helps us make more excellent content just like this.